Never mind, I'll be okay

M. Ballard

Printed in the United States of America

Cover Design: Tanya Scott
Editor: Carla DuPont
Illustration: Tanya Scott

ISBN 13: **978-1-949191-08-0**
ISBN 10: 1-949191-08-7

Jeanius Publishing LLC
430 Lee Blvd
Lehigh Acres, FL 33936

For more information, please visit:
Jeaniuspublishing.com

never mind, i'll be okay

m. ballard

to the ones who believed in us.

trigger warning:

talk of sexual assault

eating disorders

and self-harm.

other books by m. ballard

Delicate Thoughts

i am trying my best these days
to be all light and no pain

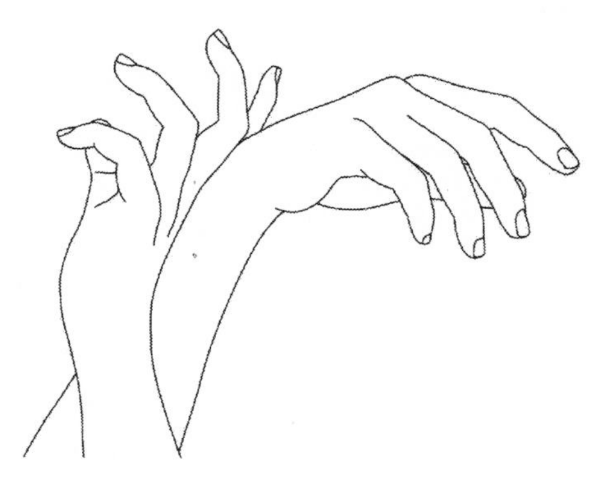

today my therapist asked me how i was feeling and i always tell her *good* or *fine*, but i know she wants more so i tell her i haven't thought about hurting myself lately--because i know that's what she cares about most. and then i tell her my body still bothers me and i think i look fat in pictures and i know that sounds extremely superficial and dumb but i can't help it. and how i've been thinking
about HIM lately; the man who i was so hopelessly in love with and how i can't seem to stop dreaming about him; and how sometimes i dial his number but never hit call.
or how i close my blinds when it starts to get dark because sunsets always remind me of him.
or how i always complain about not having friends but when i do get one i shut them out until they completely give up on me and go away forever. but i tell her despite all these

things i'm still breathing and somehow that is beautiful and my pain makes good poetry. she smiles and nods and tells me that i'm doing something right; by turning my pain into something positive, and that i shouldn't be so afraid to watch sunsets anymore.

never mind, i'll be okay

3 pm i walk to the fridge
no i can't have anything i just look
but i'm so hungry
so i sleep
hoping the sunlight fills me up
6 pm i wake
still hungry
so i sleep some more
and i know my body is a temple
but i want that temple to be thin
i had always pitied girls like this
so how did i become it
how did i let the sickness win

and when i am breaking
hold me
all i ask is you hold me

the irony in having men say
that the thing they find perfect
the thing they can't
keep their hands off
the thing they can't
stop staring at
is the exact thing
that is breaking you

- hating your body

how could i be yours
when i am still learning
how to be mine

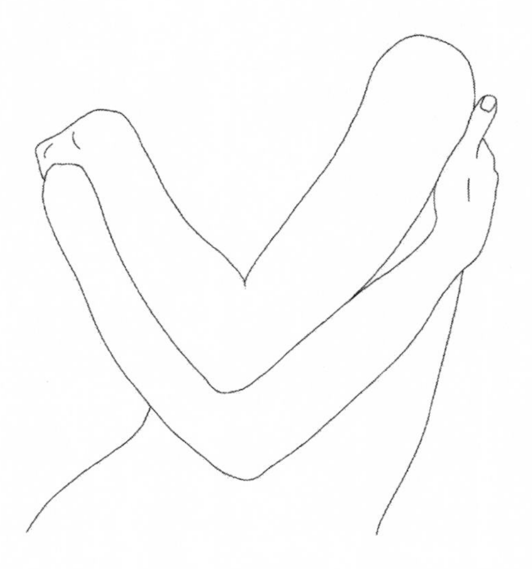

your skin
on my skin
became addicting
i did not know i was capable
of feeling so much pleasure
it was otherworldly
it was more than just physical
it was slightly spiritual
the way we worked together
in unison
to reach the same point
that feeling saved me
and i swore to God that night we said goodbye
i cried myself to sleep
because the only time i ever loved my body
was when it was underneath yours
and i knew i would never
feel that feeling again
at least not with you;
a least not for a very long time

poetry is not all about flowers
and pretty words
sometimes you have to
tell the cold hard ugly truth
the things that damaged you
the things that made you

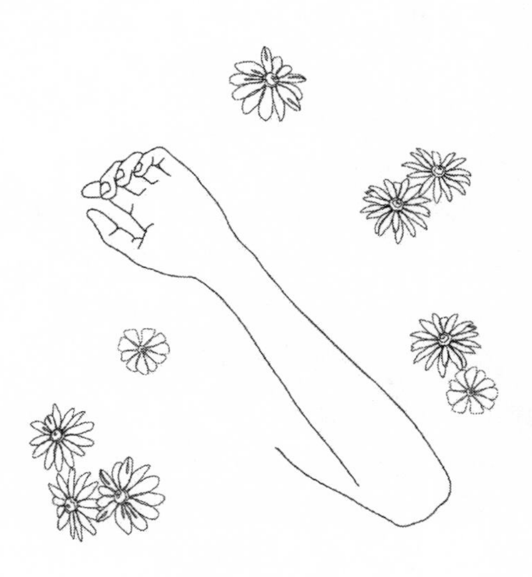

when you kill someone
you take their life
when you sexually
assault someone
you take their soul

you don't know
how badly
i need you
to steal me
from myself

my body
is not yours
to touch
and fondle
it is not your playground
i am not your toy
and no, i don't care if you think
i *asked for it*
by the garments i wear
please keep your hands
off this body
unless i grant you permission

sometime ago
i lost a piece of me
and every time i retrace
my steps
to look for it
it always leads me
back to you

one day you can't get out of bed. it feels like you're dying and if you don't dig yourself out of early morning grave, you'll be late for something important. what if you could be in two different places at the same time? but you can't move. the child in you is frozen. stuck in the corner of a room filled with nothing but the sound of your parents yelling at each other. they called it the living room, but you know that’s where they slowly killed all the love they had. but what if you could turn back the hands of the clock to when they still held hands and each other?

you wreck me
you make me question
borders of my existence
you wreck me in two
i seek shelter
under bridges

you wreck me

please do it again

never mind, i'll be okay

i figured out a few of my issues
but not sure of the remedy
i know it's not another body
or a bottle of liquor

but i still want it

i am trying to figure out
this life and why i belong here
not sure how i
turned out like this
i had a pretty normal childhood
i used to not talk a lot
and now i am just making up
for lost time
trying to get all these words out
of my head and onto paper

lately i've been finding out things
like how my father is not my real father
and how my mother kept him secret
locked up in her brain
now i am half of a person i don't know
25 years down the drain

i don't like this
but i do like this
there's something
appealing about it
this fear of the unknown
my heart beating hard in my chest

i figured out a few of my issues
but i don't know the remedy

i guess this will have to do for now

growing up
my mother taught me
how to put on lipstick
and do my hair
and dress up nice
so i can feel beautiful

but she failed to teach me
how to feel beautiful
without all of those things

how silly of me to try to
plant gardens in your chest
and try to get you to love me
when i didn't even love myself
i am truly sorry for giving you
the burden of trying to fix
a broken human being

the marks i put on myself
were not for you
or for anyone else
i did not want your pity
(i did not want you to notice)
they were for me
a reminder that i had no control
over you
and how you felt about me
or *anything,* really--
but i'll always have control over
my body
no matter what happens
i'll always have control
over one thing
and somehow
this was enough
to keep me going
somehow
this was enough
to keep me sane

i want to tell you--
how my body looks to me;
how much i ate or didn't
how much i exercised or didn't
i did not eat, or eat
to get your attention
i needed to eat nothing
to eat everything
to get rid of it all in
any way possible
this body is my loneliness
a shameful secret
i know you are not supposed
to comment on my body
but i want to share these fears
which have
haunted me for years

baby can't you see
we are making a mess
of each other

never mind, i’ll be okay

lately i've been craving a lot more
than this skin
i've been craving a lot more
than this breath
these bones
i want more than this
there has got to be more than this

i am almost certain
that a tiny piece of me
will always be yours
until the end of time

i had you once. i tasted you and i could barely handle it. i could still feel our breath between the cracks of our lips as they touched, so warm and sickly sweet. i could remember how that feeling soothed me and i knew i would do anything to keep you safe; too bad you didn't keep me safe. too bad you didn't see that i was burning for you in more ways than one. we wanted love and we got it, but we also got pain. because that's how it goes, right? a never-ending cycle. we love and then we hurt and keep doing it until we find The One. you won't stop me from keep trying. i won't ever stop seeking out love.
i had you once.
and i lost you.
but i will keep going.

how many times do i have to keep
knocking on your door to realize
love doesn't live there anymore

-how many times will i keep
hurting myself

never mind, i'll be okay

i know i can be quite
crass sometimes
i'm sure you did not forget
but i often still think about
your hands around my neck

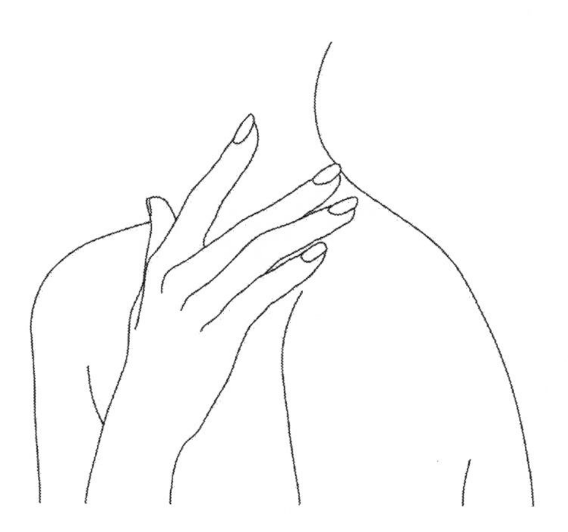

i have birthed so many poems
about you that you have become
an extended part of me
that i no longer want
but i so tragically need

i was not prepared for you
to come like a thief in the night
and take all of me
and never return again

but my darling;
the thought of you moving on--
it hurts
it hurts
it hurts

never mind, i’ll be okay

i need to stop living inside of you
and realize that your body is a war zone
and it isn't safe for me there anymore

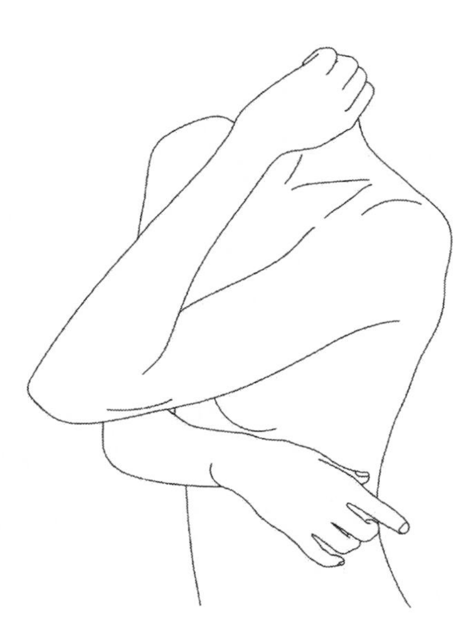

wouldn't even flinch
if you held a knife
up to my neck
baby you've been
hurting me
for too long

so tell me how it feels
that i know all the words
to take you apart

you know when you look
at something for too long
it stops making sense

well that's how it felt with you

never mind, i'll be okay

when 2 a.m arrives
this restless heart
and these idle hands
will always reach for you

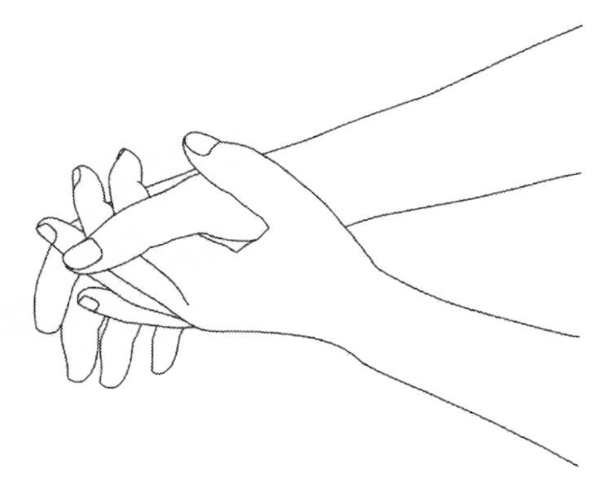

i wish my words meant
something to you
other than a sign of craziness
and another reason to leave

-my anger was a sign of love

never mind, i'll be okay

and if you whispered
sweet-nothings in my ear
and trailed kisses down my neck
would i shatter into pieces
or would it make me whole again

you cannot be just halfway mine
you might as well not be here at all

sometimes; i can't remember how to write. but then i look at you and it all just comes to me like second nature.
sometimes; i can't remember what to do with my hands, but then i look at your throat and know i want to grip it tightly until you know what it feels like to not breathe for a while. until you know what it feels like to be me.

sometimes; i can't remember how to walk because my feet have cinderblocks on them and these demons are pulling at me. but then i remember you're on the other side waiting so i get the strength to run. and when i get there your hands are shaking but i will still always hand you my heart.

sometimes; i can't remember how to sleep but then you call me to ask if you can come over and when you leave two hours later i feel like there is no soul left in me and i lay there naked wondering how i got a boyfriend who is only half mine.
i am broken. and i am so, so tired.

sometimes; i can't remember how to speak but now that you're asking me what's wrong everything is flowing out of my mouth like a river or a stream. i'm tired of giving the easy answer. no more shortcuts. i will tell you everything that is wrong with me, since you asked.
pull up a chair, it's going to be a while.

-when he asks you what's wrong

i have gone back and forth
between loving you and hating you
for so long
that lines are now blurred and
it all just feels the same

(it all just feels like pain)

never mind, i'll be okay

and even though you hurt me
i want to rip open my chest
and let you live there forever

i stripped the bed
and threw away the sheets
we once shared
because no matter
how many times
i washed them
i could still smell your scent
and it always left me up at night
wondering what became of you

never mind, i'll be okay

darling;
please don't say we are done
i have so much left to give

so what's there to say
other than
you are
and always will be
in my veins

never mind, i'll be okay

soft hands
bright smile
eyes that promised nothing
but temporary love

i knew i was in for a world full of hurt
(but i let it happen anyways)

your smile softened the blow but it still hurt

never mind, i'll be okay

your words slip out of
your mouth like silk
and i caught every single one
and swallowed it whole

and despite the pain they are causing me
i am still hungry for more

i'll kiss the doubt off your lips if you
kiss the worry off mine

he lit a match to the green that sat untouched
on the coffee table. we expressed ourselves that
night, our uncovered insanities as we covered our
skin with soft sheets.

secrets we thought we'd never tell were written
all over those bedroom walls; laughs, cries, lies.
it all collapsed on us that night. i knew his body,
but now i knew his mind, too. and to tell you
the truth, i was terrified. not of him, but of his
abilities to fix me.

i bathe in anguish accompanied with a cup of coffee
to soothe the penetrated pain in the morning.
darkness was all i've ever ben fed. his presence was
a burning almost tingling feeling; a slow but
rather soothing sensation. looking back on it now,
i might have just loved him.

i thought i was done
writing about you
but your words
and your hurt
keep spilling over
on every page

-these are still delicate thoughts

and i wanted so desperately
for you to see the good in me
i hurt myself trying to
get you to love me back
no good could ever come from that

don't look at me like that boy,
you make me crumble-- *don't you get it?*
you were the one who needed saving
the most but you would never admit it

what i realized is you can't
be someone's saving grace
if they don't want saving
and the taste of their lips at midnight
will only temporarily satisfy
your craving

-it will only stop hurting for a while
until they leave again

my love is big and mighty
look at it
the way it unfurls
unfolds
stretches out to the sky

i'm sorry you could not handle it

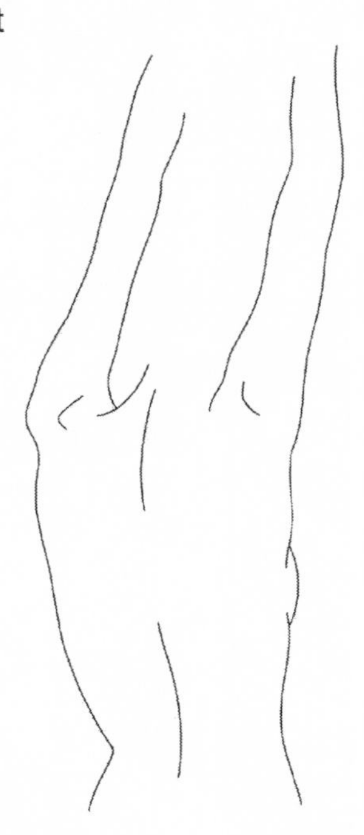

there's no running away from it
this is how we are conditioned
love will be our downfall--
until the very
end
of time

they keep saying i have changed
and i cannot tell you
how happy i am
that they are right

i want you to tell me where you've been and where you plan to go. i want you to spill your heart out into my hands; i want to rifle through the contents of it. i want to know what you were like as a child. i want to know everyone you've loved before me, because i know they were the ones who made you who you are. i want to greet all of your demons. i want to get to know every one, even the ones that you've hidden away for so long that they are coated in dust.

tell me. tell me who you are when no one is around. tell me what you become. tell me who you are when no one is looking. tell me, does your here beat different at 2 am like mine? let me get to know that person. open up to me. i promise i won't run away. i want to know you, more than anything in this world. i want to know how to keep you.
i want to know how to love you right.

been filling up my cup with love
and it's been overflowing
ever since i met you

never mind, i'll be okay

12 am midnight
everything i need is here
in this bed
in your arms
everything i need is here
everything i need is you

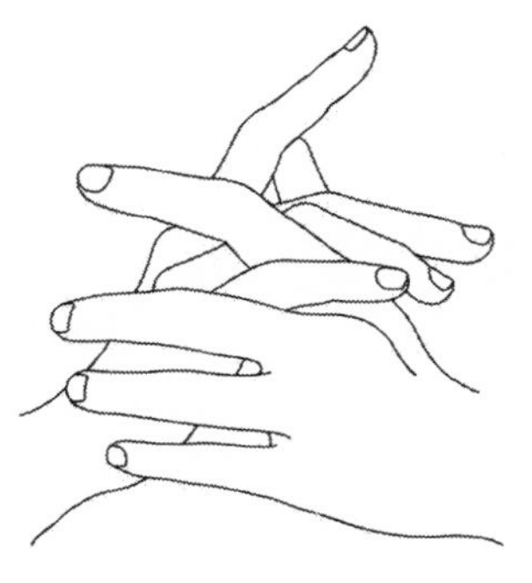

you have the kind of love that
wraps itself around throats
instead of fingers

never mind, i'll be okay

those eyes of yours
they set me ablaze
hot white fire
that'll keep me warm
for days

you make it so easy for me to love you. with those soft eyes and that killer smile. as soon as you walk into the room my temperature rises and before we know it you are laying me down on silky bedsheets, our limbs are entangled and we're both bathed in moonlight. i know you love beautiful things. and so do i. i love you so much and i can't help to look at you that way. i mean, there's art everywhere. and i know i'd be able to tell you're a poem just by looking at you, even if i didn't know how to read. because that's how much i adore you.

i want to take you to thailand because i know you want to go there and we'd slow dance under the bamboo forests and kiss in the warm rain. i never got love until i met you. and now i know what it is. that giddy feeling. that knot you get in the pit of your stomach. this love i have for you is insurmountable it's almost scary. so scary that you can feel it in your bones. but i don't want to run away from it. i only want to embrace it. i only want to hold it closer. because this is the way that i love.

never mind, i'll be okay

broken looks good on you
but i'd rather see you whole

in this book of life
i will highlight the pages
i fell in love with you
and come back to it on rainy days

-reminiscing

so many things i want
to pretend with you
as if your world had
any chance at colliding
with mine
as if planets really did
pass by
and wave at each other

still i daydream
of wearing you
like a ring around saturn
and maybe letting you
disrupt my atmosphere

it's not love
if it doesn't hurt
just a little bit
when you look at them

because the thought
of losing them forever

i fell in love with a boy
that turned out to be
the answer to all my prayers
and when they ask me
about religion all i can
think about is him

you move with such ease and grace
i am almost certain that you are an angel

never mind, i'll be okay

i can't stare at the stars
and not think of your eyes
and other things
that would cause
a room of people
to turn and stare and worship
in awe of your beauty

i remember it so clearly;
the feeling that i got when we
first locked eyes
i've been carrying that feeling
with me ever since

there is an art to holding
the someone you love
you will reach for them as if
you are painting
the very air with abstract hands
you will become
tangled, messy,
beautiful
together you will find a home
and sometimes;
your hands will bleed sunsets
and forests
and waterfalls
and cherry blossoms
and every color in between

ever since you touched me
i haven't been the same since

i've stayed up so many nights
professing my love for you
that i'm convinced that the moon
and the stars and the planets
all know your name

-3 a.m. knows you so well

i cannot heal you
but i can keep you company
and sit with you
in your brokenness
for a while

never mind, i'll be okay

i know i said no more
but *my God*--
those eyes;
they just pull me
right back in

i'm up thinking about you
and how you smelled like stars
and a little bit of honeydew
how your eyelashes touched
the bottoms of your cheeks
when you looked down
and how when you smiled
i felt like i might drown

how did you do that

i'm convinced that he was just
a figment of my imagination
because there's no way a boy
who held the sun like that
actually exists

there's no question that it was you
who brought out the poet in me

my love could heal you
and break you
both at the same time
it'll keep your head calm
it'll keep your heart wild

i want the kind

of love

i can sink my

teeth into

there's no containing the love
i have for you, boy
i could feel the love i have for you
in the back of my throat
and it is pouring out of me
i will keep loving you
until it consumes me whole

i don't care how long it's been
these hands
 have memorized
every inch of your skin

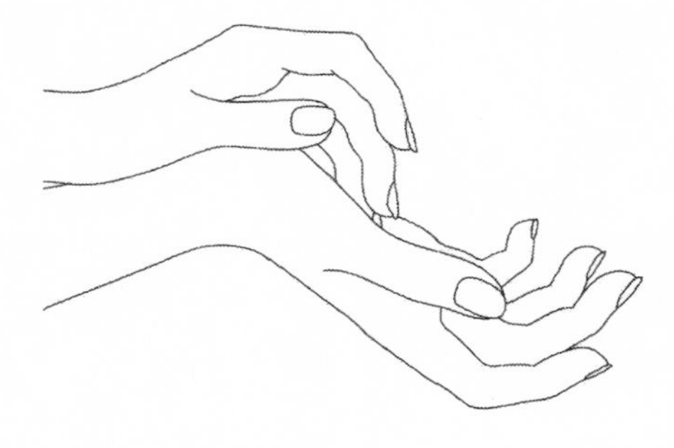

never mind, i'll be okay

when you smile it slices
through to the very marrow
of my bones

-every single time

my fingertips were lost in the warmth of his hand. when i rested against him, i felt like i could fall into his body. the flame of the candle flickered in two, and electric crimson warnings, shined bright around me. the scare was fierce, and i will not back down. challenge accepted, my dear gemini.

see, what he may not realize, is that *i know him.* i know him well enough to not be afraid of him. i've studied his every word – even the unsaid. i know the way his brain works and how his mind is beautiful and *limitless*.
i've taken his energy and have given him my own; the exchange had so much bright, white light to offer. i know his soul, it's familiar.

if he really thinks he can scare me away, he is sorely mistaken. no one is scarier than the depths of my own soul. i will always rise through death, heartbreak, and anything else that could cause destruction to my self. that's what birds of flames do – we rise from our ashes into a rebirth; an awakening.

every story written, or told, has been manifested by it's author. i am the author of this story. i too have a powerful mind and a strong energy connection to the universe, dear gemini. i asked, and the universe has delivered. i've been on this incredible soul journey so i can understand myself better, love myself more, and heal my soul of all it's darkest parts. i've been preparing for *this*. for *him.* he may not realize it yet,

never mind, i'll be okay

but he's been doing the same for *me*. i'm *not* like all of the other girls.

love me
even when i ask you not to
even when i am upset
and there's more anger in my eyes
than you can handle
love me
even when my hands are
shaking from sadness
even when you feel like giving up;
find some hope
and love me
love me
love me

and oh,
how beautiful
how after all that heartbreak
after you thought
you couldn't go on
the way the world
folds you up
sticks you in its pocket
and carries you into the new day

you have gone many days
before you met them
so you can survive when
they are gone

i've been beaten
broken down
shattered
and put back together
imperfectly with time

and i'm learning to deal
with this body
it's the only one that i have
and even though there is darkness
in places where there shouldn't be
i know that this magic
inside of me will bloom
so beautifully

-give me more time

finally found the love i was looking for
tucked between my own ribs

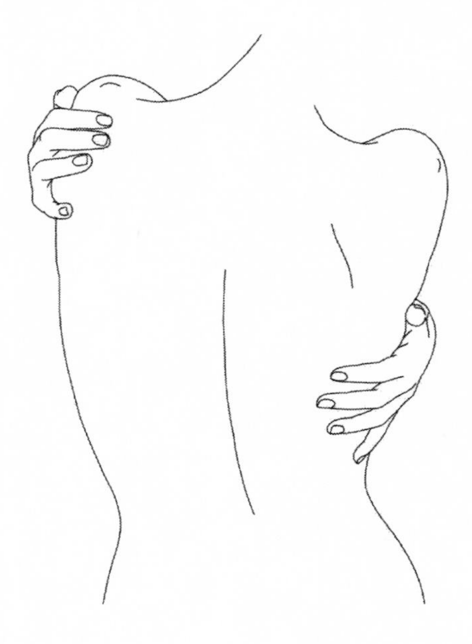

i can think of many
reasons why i write
but none of them
are more clearer
than to just find
some hope

hoping this light can carry me into the new day

she held everything
in the palm of her hands
she was unstoppable
and could do whatever
she dreamed of

she was
her own kind of magic

i will keep writing until love has
stopped radiating from all corners
of my body from the tips of my toes;
to the very ends of my fingertips
i will keep writing until the words
stop flowing so easily
and the bags under my eyes
have been emptied
of all the love and pain

and when those are empty
i will dig up some more love

some more pain (because it is worth it)
and fill them back up
and i will keep writing
(i will keep writing until the death of me.)

in the end honesty
and kindness
are the only things that matter
if you have those
everything else will follow

there is pain here
but there is also love
i promise
there is so much love

i feel myself changing into something;
i don't know into what but i hope it is
some kind of beautiful

and i know i am
often sad but
some days there
is more hope in
my bones than
i know what
to do with

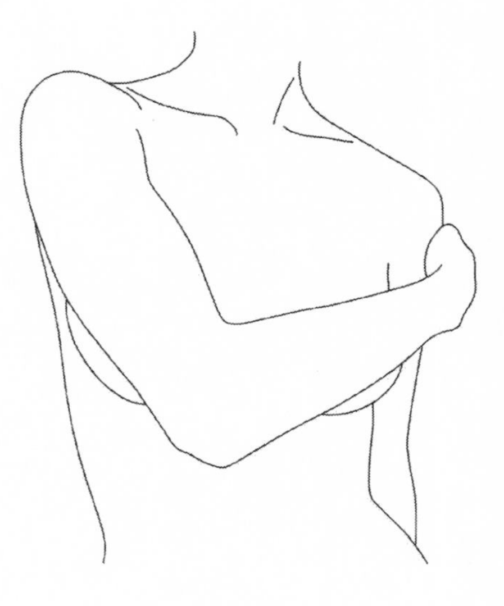

i promise it won't always feel like this
i promise that one day the storm
brewing inside that chest of yours
will finally calm

instead of lovers
i will fill this void
in my chest with light
and hopefully that will
be enough for now
until i find the one
who is worthy to stay

lay your burdens down
and get some rest tonight
for the morning will
bring you peace

oh, but how bold
and courageous of us
that we keep on loving
even after our hearts
were broken

this peace can be yours
if you want it
it has always been yours
all along

what if this is all
we were meant to be
just souls passing by
for a fleeting moment
in time
to hopelessly
recklessly
fall apart
and then rise from the ashes
as if none of it ever happened

-survival

never mind, i'll be okay

she's got warmth
the sun knows nothing about

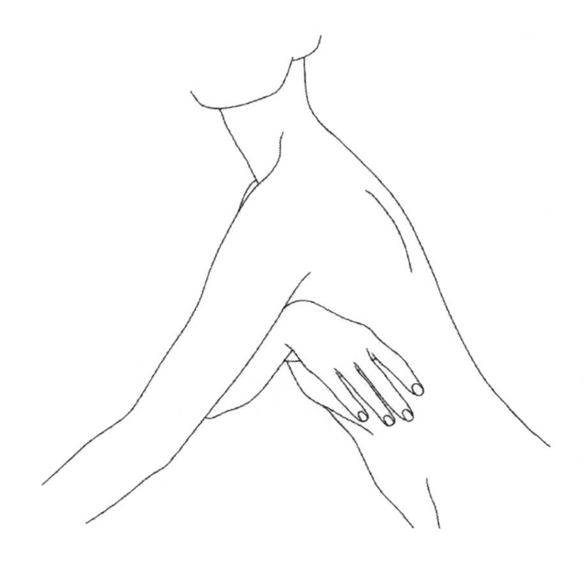

my dearest love,

it's no surprise you fell in love with me, it's an easy thing to do. i'm smart, clever, witty, so sarcastic that you have to question it sometimes, hell – even i have to; and i make you feel like you are the most special person in the world. that's because you are.
i'll help you strive to be who you want to be, because i fully support you and all of your ventures. i want nothing more from you than the unconditional love that you have in your heart. the love that you keep sealed up,
because you're afraid of the pain that has happened to you in the past.

i want you to know that while it's easy to be in love with me now, it won't always be easy. as much as i try to have balance in my life, it's usually a facade. deep down inside i'm full of whirlwinds that are strong enough to pick you up and make you fall flat on your face if you don't brace yourself. preparation for these whirlwinds are not easy though, as they come out of nowhere.

there is an ugly side of me. the words that come out of my mouth are often times unfiltered, sharp, and carry a sting. i speak before i think, and when i speak out of anger, it's not always how i really feel. in order to avoid this, i have to sit and think… alone. so when i turn around and walk away from a conversation going south, let me be free. do not chase me, or i will run. i promise you that once i think and get my thoughts in order, we will talk like adults. i don't like yelling and fighting.

you have to understand and be willing to embrace all of my scars. while they do not define who i am, they have helped me develop into who i have become. i'm forever evolving and my higher self is only getting brighter, you'll never have to be in the dark again with me by your side.
it's important for you to allow me to make myself number one. you will always be second to me, and it's not out of selfishness, it's out of the selfless love for myself i have been working on. i can never be tamed, as my heart is wild; filled with passion, it will love you fiercely.
my loyalty to you is deeply rooted. i will care for you, wash your socks and underwear, and cook you meals, but don't ever hold expectations for these gifts, because that's the moment when i will disappoint you.

let's know each other's past, and share story time, but let's not dwell on what has happened and instead let's focus on what is happening. we can daydream about the future, and imagine what life will be like, but keep the focus on the way my hand feels in your hand in this very moment.

my dearest love, you never have to worry about breaking my heart because the heart can't be broken and if you bruise my

ego, that's okay, it's a reminder that i don't need the ego anyway. i won't get jealous and i hope the same from you. i don't deal well with it. the fact that i'm
a super flirt will never change. know in your heart that it is you i love and free yourself of any insecurities that will make you think otherwise. you are my King. know that when you stare into my eyes, each time, i open my soul to you, deeper and deeper and deeper.

i've faced what's in there, and though it can be scary, don't worry, i'll protect you. i've slain most of the dragons that once hid in the darkest caverns of my soul and i'll continue to slay more as i grow.
please know that i will always appreciate you and everything you do, even though i may not say it all of the time.

sometimes i get busy with so many things at one time that i forget to take a breath. when you see this happening, don't hesitate to slow me down with a kiss. my dearest love, whoever you may be, just remember; meeting you was the day that changed my life forever. for the better.
i am as lucky to have found you as you are to have found me.
i will always do my best to understand every part of you, and i will love you unconditionally.

one day someone will
mention their name
and you will feel
no bitterness
no hatred
no hurt in your heart
and that's how you know
you have found inner peace

all of us were born so pure--filled with the highest vibrations and the best intentions. yet through hurt, programming, and environmental influences we forget who we truly are. awakening isn't gaining something new. it's letting go of what we are not. it's shedding off old skin, old programming, old ways of thinking. whenever somebody is hurtful i remember to love them even that much more. to love them is to remind them of what they truly are. they are truly love. we are truly love. you are truly love; i love unconditionally--knowing that it is my job as a member of this universe to remind others of the glowing essence they truly are.

never mind, i'll be okay

when you find that you are
losing hope
you need to find that little bit
of light inside of you
hold on to it tight
and let it get you through the night

-it will be better in the morning

she's made entirely out of brushstrokes
yet she doesn't even know she is art

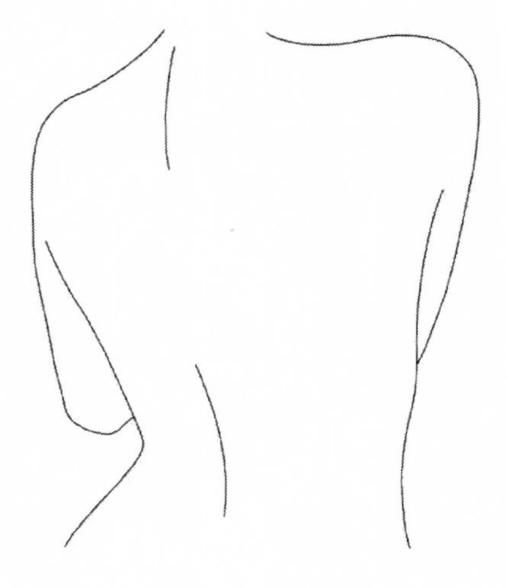

don't you dare think you are less than
because of how they left you

-you are more than enough

i am starting to think that
all this breaking was worth it
because now i know
what i am capable of

-never mind, i'll be okay

never mind, i'll be okay

please do not be so reckless

with yourself

you are all

that you have

sometimes it's best to just BE. be able to learn to love yourself through the upsetting silence of others. be able to find compassion for yourself through the lack of compassion of others. be able to listen to what your soul needs, versus the deep desires of your ego.
be able to grow from your roots, into the highest heavens. be able to separate yourself from the world of 3D. just be able to… BE… and let BE… even if it means being alone for a while.

never mind, i'll be okay

i cannot tell you where i am going
but i promise it will be better than this

you can feel the pain
if you want to
feel it
for however long you need to
but remember to set it free
when you are done

there's a soft violence about you. i can't really tell if it's the pressure that you're putting on yourself or the pressure your parents have been putting on you lately. i see the way they look at you. like they're disappointed with all of your actions. i can tell that there's a storm brewing behind those soft eyes of yours.
you're desperately looking for someone who understands you. who loves you and all of your flaws. you need to stop looking and let it come to you. stop stressing.

whatever it is, let it go. don't you know what the best is yet to come? i can tell you're tired.
get some rest, you did your best today.

the end

Made in the USA
Monee, IL
08 May 2020